YIELDING YOUR WILL TOTALLY TO GOD

BARBARA L. LINDSEY

Yielding Your Will Totally To God

Copyright © 2005

Barbara L. Lindsey

ISBN: 978-0-9787739-0-8

Dedication

I dedicate this book to my Father, God, who gave me this talent, and to my LORD and Savior, Jesus Christ. To my mentor, (the late) Dr. Annie G. Vaughn, who asked me a question in Sunday school: Sister Barbara, "What is your talent"? I also dedicate this book to my Pastors, Apostle Larry N. & Evangelist Sarah D. Crosby who prayed for me and brought this gift forth. Last, but not least I dedicate this book to my son, George F. Brewer, who encouraged me to finish college.

ACKNOWLEDGEMENTS

I give my Father, God all the glory and honor for the great things he has done and is doing in my life. I thank God for all the prayers of the saints at Haven of Truth World Wide Deliverance Churches INC. Special thanks to the Author, Sister Nichelle Conner, of the book, "My Ram Was in the Thicket who the Lord sent from Lubbock, Texas to Rockingham, North Carolina to help make my dream come true. Thanks to my daughter-in law, Chilite D. Brewer, who introduced me to Sister Conner, who gave me some tips that she learned as an author.

INDEX

Introduction

I'm asking every believer in the body of Christ just for a moment to empty yourselves of the things you have learned about the "Soul" of man and open your hearts and minds as you read this book. I believe God will enlighten the eyes of our understanding. This book will help the unbeliever to surrender their lives to Christ and cause them to gain the victory over the fear of backsliding.

I'm writing this book "Yielding your will totally to God" because I've seen so many believers through the years yield to God in fasting, prayer, and studying God's word only to receive the anointing for their gift (ministry).

Yet I saw them fall flat on their faces because they couldn't live what they preached. We, humans, have a way of putting the cart before the horse in almost everything we set our minds to do. We want things in a hurry and don't want to prepare for the long haul, but now we must find our way back so we can put the horse before the cart.

This book is not about ministry, or our ministry gifts it's about ministering to the Lord in our daily walk. When the body of Christ, understands kingdom principles and how to yield their wills totally to God then ministry and everything else He has for them will come to pass.

(KJV-6: 33) "But seek ye first the kingdom of God, and all his righteousness; and all these things will be added unto you." Reader stop saying things like "I'm waiting on God" to heal me, to bless me etc., because He has given us everything that pertains to life and godliness. (KJV-I Peter 1:3)

Have you ever wonder why you lose more victories since you became a born-again believer than you did in your life before salvation? Have you prayed, fasted, and even read the Bible faithfully and still you feel like you are defeated in your Christian walk? Have you ever wonder why the wicked prosper, and Christians who have Heaven's best struggle spiritually, emotionally and even financially.

Let's be honest with ourselves and with God and He can help us! If your answer is yes to any of these questions you are on your way to living a victorious life through Christ Jesus. This book will encourage every Christian to triumph in his or her daily walk of faith. It will open up your understanding of what it means to be made in the image of God and after His likeness. I believe God by faith that this book will be a blessing to many when people began to understand that God has done everything He is going to do through His Son, Christ Jesus, and it's up to them to make things happen in their lives. Remember there are three kinds of people: Those who make it happen, those who watch it happen, and those who ask what happen?

Reader a word to the wise is sufficient: Many people that are not saved have yielded their "Will" to God to get the blessings of God and have received them. Healing and financial blessings are in the atonement through the blood of Jesus, and the sinner can receive them if they follow the "Laws of the Spirit."

Remember God rains on the just as well as the unjust. Sinner, God never said you have to choose healing or finances because He has given you all things through his Son, Jesus, which included the Salvation of your souls. Matthew 16:26 KJV "For what will it profit a man to gain the whole world and lose his own soul? Or what shall a man give in exchange for his soul?"

If you are not saved or born-again take a moment and ask God to forgive you of your sins, and invite Him into your heart. All have sin and come short of the glory of God. There isn't a sin that Jesus' blood can't wash away and make the sinner every whit whole. He is knocking at your heart's door. Do it today. Don't put it off another day; our life is but a vapor, and tomorrow is not promised. (KJV-Romans 3:23;Revelation 3:20)

Chapter 1

MAN MADE IN THE IMAGE OF GOD

In Genesis 1:26 KJV "And God said, Let us make man in our image, after our likeness: and let them have dominion over the fish of the sea, and the fowl of the air, and over the cattle, and over all the earth, and over every creeping thing that creepeth upon the earth." (Genesis 1:27;I Thessalonians 5:23)

Note that God said; Let us make man in our image, after our likeness. What does this verse mean? Does it mean that we resemble God? To give you a better understanding of this verse let's go to I John 5:7 KJV "For there are three that bear record in heaven, the Father, the Word, and the Holy Ghost: and these three are one."

The Godhead bodily is Triune. Man who is made in the image of God is also triune. Many false religion deny the "Trinity. They will either leave Jesus out of the Godhead bodily or they will leave out the Holy Ghost.

Jesus was the "Word" that God spoke before He became flesh. He always existed for he was in the beginning. (KJV-John 1:14)

Concerning God, the Holy Ghost, this is His dispensation. Some read the book of Acts and call it the Acts of the Apostles, but without the power of the Holy Ghost the Apostles couldn't do any mighty works or acts.

The scriptures in Matthew the third chapter show a glimpse of all three together during the baptism of Jesus. While John is baptizing Jesus, the Spirit is resting upon Jesus like a dove, and the Father is showing His approval as He speaks from heaven. (K J V-Matthew 3:16,17)

Adam was triune: for he was "Spirit", "Soul", and "Body." (KJV-I Thessalonians 5:23) Adam was made in the image of God and after His likeness. He was the god of this world. (KJV-I Corinthians 4:4) God had given him authority and dominion over everything in the Earth.

The Spirit of God dwelt in Adam's spirit, which made him God Conscious. Romans 8:9 KJV says, "But ye are not in the flesh, but in the Spirit, if so be that the Spirit of God dwell in you. Now if any man have not the Spirit of Christ, he is none of his."

His Soul is where the seat of his emotions, appetites, self-will, will, intellect, reasoning (imaginations) dwelt that made him Self-Conscious. The Body houses both the Spirit of God, and the Soul. This is what it means to be made in the image of God and after His likeness.

Paul, the Apostle, said that we have this treasure in earthen vessels. He was speaking of the Holy Ghost that resides in the believer's temple. Later in this book we will show you that the sinner is also "Spirit", "Soul", and "Body". The Bible doesn't tell us how long Adam walked and talked with God in complete harmony before he rebelled. However, the Bible gives us insight concerning the authority that God gave Adam when He gave him dominion over all things in the earth, and he wasn't limited in what he could imagine in his soul to speak or do. For Paul, the Apostle, wrote "I can do all things through Christ which strengtheneth us." (KJV-Philippians-4:13) For God created him an intellectual and spiritual being and he named all the animals and everything upon the earth. (KJV-Genesis 2:19)

C. I. Scofield D.D. said This is divine Magna Charta for all true scientific and material progress. Man began with a mind that was perfect in its finite capacity for learning, but he did not begin knowing all secrets of the universe. He is commanded to "subdue" i.e. acquire a knowledge of and mastery over his material environment, to bring its element into the service of the race. To add to this statement none of God's creation is omniscient.

Adam could have walked and talked with God a long time before he sinned. Genesis 3:8 KJV "And they heard the voice of the Lord God walking in the garden in the cool of the day: and Adam and his wife hid themselves from the presence of the Lord God amongst the trees of the garden."

I believe before God gave Adam his help meet he walked and talked with God and was in complete harmony with Him. Adam,

9

had a Covenant relationship with God as His son, and they enjoyed their fellowship until one day he (Adam) broke the Covenant. God also prepared Adam for his wife. He taught Adam what it meant to be head and have dominion over everything in the earth, and he taught him how to protect and provide. God never gives us anything until he prepares us for the blessing. There wasn't anything that Adam couldn't achieve because he was made in the image of God, and after His likeness. He was like God in every way in that he could speak life to every situation and it would come to pass. God's intention for Adam was for him to live for eternity so he created him in His image. There's no death in God only life, and it was the will of God that there be no death in Adam.

God must established authority on the earth and men must yield their wills totally to God. Yielding helps us to obey God's word, and it causes us to walk in complete harmony with Him. We must understand that obedience is learned through the things we suffer. We see in this scripture that even Jesus had to learn obedience by the things he suffered. (KJV-Hebrews 5:8)
I will talk about the last Adam in the final chapter of this book. God tested both Lucifer, first ruler, of the Earth, and Adam, the second ruler, and they failed their test. In order for authority to be established in the earth obedience must be an act of our will. The "Act of the Will" clearly states I'm serving God because I love him and I choose too. God wants us to serve him because we love him. The scriptures told us we should love the LORD thy God with all our heart, soul, and might. (KJV-Deuteronomy 6:5) He made us free mortal agents giving us the power of choice. (KJV-Deuteronomy 30:19) If authority is not established, and the creature made subject to the creator then there will be chaos in the earth. Elohim, is our Creator, and He knows what's best for us.

Chapter 2
Lucifer, First Ruler of the Earth

Let's go back before the creation of Adam so we can gain insight on the plan of Satan, who comes to steal, kill, and destroy our souls. (KJV-John 10:10) Satan, whose name was Lucifer, a created Archangel, which covered the throne of God, and who was the first ruler, of the Earth before God's man, Adam. This is found in Isaiah 14:12-14 and Ezekiel 28:11-16 verses in the King James Version. Stop for a moment and read those scriptures.

To establish authority in the Heavens and Earth God must put His creatures to a test. The purpose was to prove both angelic and human beings. Each creature must be loyal, obedient, and walk in complete harmony with God. God gives the answers to every test in His word so we are without excuse. God, doesn't owe anyone an explanation because He is Sovereign, and He is our "Creator" therefore he knows what's best for his creation.

A test was necessary because He must prove whether they would be loyal and faithful to him not just for then, but for eternity. Without authority being established in Heaven, and Earth there will be chaos. Just think for a moment how many deaths would occur if a person drove his or her vehicle seventy-five miles in a thirty-five mile zone. Lucifer was given rule over the earth, and he was to rule in complete harmony with His Creator, God.

Ezekiel 28:14 KJV " Thou art the anointed cherub that covereth; and I have set thee so: thou wast upon the holy mountain of God; thou hast walked up and down in the midst of the stones of fire. 15 verse Thou wast perfect in thy ways from the day that thou wast created, till iniquity was found in thee." It was God who created Lucifer, and gave him authority and dominion to rule the earth. God gave Angels, (Celestial), and Human beings a will, and he made them free mortal agents. He gave them a choice. They were not robots. The Lord wants us to love and obey him, because we choose too.

The Lord tested Lucifer, Ruler, of the Earth even though it doesn't say what his test was, but we know he failed the test. This is not scriptural but I believe he was tested with the tree of knowledge of good and evil in the first Earth that he ruled during the Dispensation of Angels that's my theory. I came to that conclusion from two things: First there was no evil in Heaven or Earth, but the tree of knowledge of good and evil which I believe there was one on both Earth.

Ecclesiastes 3:15 KJV "That which hath been is now; and that which is to be hath already been; and God requireth that which is past." Lucifer was also in a garden; Ezekiel called it "Eden the garden of God." Second, God created everything and pronounced that it was good. When Satan tempted Eve through the serpent how would he know about the tree of knowledge of good and evil unless he partook of the fruit? Remember God gave Lucifer and his angels wisdom and he made Adam an intellectual being, but only God is omniscient.

Notice what God said in Genesis 3rd Chapter 22 verse KJV "And LORD God said, Behold, the man is become as one of us, to know good and evil: and now, lest he put forth his hand, and take also of the tree of life, and eat, and live forever." God in his mercy didn't want man to live in that sinful state forever so he drove him out of the Garden. Genesis 3:23-24 KJV "Therefore the Lord God sent him forth from the garden of Eden, to till the ground from whence he was taken. 24 So he drove out the man; and he placed at the east of the garden of Eden Cherubim, and a flaming sword which turned every way to keep the way of the tree of life."

Whatever the test that God gave Lucifer he failed. He failed through pride and made a decision to plan a rebellion with the third part of the angels that rebelled with him against God. Isaiah 14:13 KJV "For thou hast said in thine heart, I will ascend into heaven, I will exalt my throne above the stars of God: I will sit also upon the mount of the congregation, in the sides of the north I will ascend above the heights of the clouds; I will be like the most High."

Yielding our wills totally to God is very important. We cancel out our prayers, fasting, and studying the word of God when we don't yield our wills totally to God. The word of God talks about Lucifer's wisdom in Ezekiel 28:12. (KJV)

In fact it says he was full of wisdom, but that wasn't enough because he chose to rebel against his Creator. Remember reader, having knowledge doesn't give you power, but the Holy Ghost, He, gives us power. He also teaches us and gives us knowledge of the word of God.

Lucifer and Adam allowed their souls to make them think God was holding something back from them. The choice Lucifer made cause him to lose his position with God and he was cast out of the third heavens. (KJV-Revelation 12:7-8)

He wasn't cast on the earth at that time, he is the prince of the power of the air. Later he will be cast to the earth during the time of the anti-Christ. (KJV-Ephesians 2:2;Rev. 12:9) He still has access to come as a Son of God to present himself before God. (KJV-Job 1:6-12)

When God walked into the "Garden of Eden" to fellowship with Adam as He did previously He found him hiding from him. Genesis 3:8 KJV "And they heard the LORD God walking in the cool of the day: and Adam and his wife hid themselves from the presence of the LORD God amongst the trees of the garden." God is omniscient so He knew Adam had disobeyed Him, but God wants us to confess our sin so he can forgive us. (KJV-I John 1:9) Sin will strip you naked, and cause you to hide from your Creator. Reader, read Genesis 3:8-15 verses and you will found that God gives us a glimpse of hope for mankind. Genesis 3:15 KJV "And I will put enmity between thee and the woman, and between thy seed and her seed; it shall bruise thy head, and thou shalt bruise his heel." This was the first prophecy concerning Jesus, the last Adam, who would come and destroy the works of Satan. He will bruise his head and defeat Satan and re-gain back what the first Adam lost and reconcile man back to Himself. (Genesis 3:15; II Corinthians 5:18)

Jesus has fulfilled this prophetic word in Genesis 3:15 and many other prophecies in the Old Testament concerning man's Salvation. Satan knows he is a defeated foe, but he is not going to admit his defeat to the Christian. He will huff and puff, to make us think he has power to blow our house down, but he can't blow our house down if it's built on the word of God, a solid foundation. (Matthew 7:24-27) Satan is both God and Man's archenemy, and he knows he has but a short time. (Revelation 12:12) When Satan rebelled he found out he was no match for his Creator, Almighty God, but his goal is to steal, kill, and destroy God's most prize creation, "Man."

Chapter 3
Recreated Earth

Genesis 1:1 KJV says, "In the beginning God created the heaven and the earth." Genesis 1:2 KJV says, "And the earth was without form, and void; and darkness was upon the face of the deep. And the Spirit of God moved upon the face of the waters." We see something devastated happening in the first chapter of Genesis between the first verse and, the second verse. God created the heaven and earth, and the scriptures began to say in the next verse the earth was without form and void. In the second chapter of this book we see that Lucifer, the Archangel, ruled the earth before Adam was created by God in His own image. He failed his test and rebelled and God cast him out of heaven, and now he is the prince of the power of the air. (KJV-Ephesians 2:2)

God took the earth and shook off the inhabitants thereof, and recreated the earth and made Adam the second ruler. Isaiah 24:1 KJV "Behold, the Lord maketh the earth empty, and maketh it waste, and turneth it upside down, and scattered abroad the inhabitants thereof." The world that Lucifer ruled perished, but the earth was not destroyed it overflowed with water and the Lord maketh it waste. The Lord restored the earth that overflowed in water from Genesis 1:3-2:25. Apostle, Peter, wrote about that world that Lucifer ruled and he called it the earth that then was. Scoffers in that day were ignorant concerning God's word even as it is today. We still hear people saying, "Jesus was coming back when my grandmother was alive, and he hasn't come back yet." II Peter 3:4-8 And saying, Where is the promise of his coming? for since the fathers fell asleep, all things continue as they were from the beginning of the creation.

5th verse "For this they willingly are ignorant of, that by the word of God the heaven were of old, and the earth standing out of the water and in the water: 6th verse Whereby the world that then was, being overflowed with water perished: 7th verse But the heavens and the earth, which are now, by the same word are kept in store, reserved unto fire against the day of judgment and perdition of ungodly men. 8th verse- But, beloved, be not ignorant of this one thing, that one day is with the Lord as a thousand years, and a thousand years as one day.

Don't get Lucifer's flood confused with Noah's flood as we will referred to them as, but understand that the earth wasn't destroyed in Noah's Dispensation (Human Government). All the people and creatures were destroyed except those animals that God instructed Noah to take into the ark, along with Noah and his family members. (Genesis 7:1-9)

Genesis 6:7 KJV "And the LORD said, I will destroy man whom I have created from the face of the earth; both man, and beast, and the creeping thing, and the fowls of the air; for it repenteth me that I made them.

8th verse But Noah found grace in the eyes of the Lord." The LORD saved eight persons and the animals He instructed Noah to bring into the ark. (Genesis: 6-9 chapters).

Through the years the word of God has proven its validity, and is still standing the test of time. He has given us a "Better Covenant" that is establish upon better promises, but "Man" has ignore the lessons that the word of God teaches and has gone his own way. The "Earth" has become corrupt again as it was in the days of "Noah." Men's heart and imaginations are yet evil and we have gone astray from our Father, God, and His Son Jesus Christ. Men are yielding their wills to sin and Satan instead of God. We, Christians, are crucifying the Lord afresh with our raggedy lives. Hebrews 6:6 KJV says, "If they shall fall away, to renew them again unto repentance; seeing they crucify to themselves the Son of God afresh, and put him to an open shame."

We, born-again Christians, have the Spirit of God in us like Adam and also have the power of "Choice." Many of us (Christians) have let down our standards, and have compromised with Satan. God will renovate the present Heaven and Earth with fire and put down all rebellion. (KJV-II Peter 3:10-13)

16

God inspired Holy men to write the word of God. (KJV-II Timothy 3:16) Moses wrote the book of Genesis and God wants us to read His word and let it guide us down the right path. God is not a respecter of persons, and we must not take advantage of the grace of God, or use His grace as a license to sin because we are in the dispensation of "Grace and Truth."

A special note: The earth is not six- thousand years old as some might think, there is no number we can calculate how old the earth is, but we can use the words "beginning" and "eternity past." Remember God gave Adam, the second ruler, of the earth a six-thousand years lease of the earth.

Chapter 4
Born- again from life unto death

I preached a message some time ago and the topic was "Born-again from life unto death." Let that sink in for a moment, and I will show you what God has revealed unto me by His Spirit.

In the first chapter, I began to write that God must establish authority on the earth through obedience to His will. Adam was God's most prize creation because he was made in the image of God and after His likeness. No other creature was made in the image of God.

Genesis 1:26 KJV "And God said, Let us make man in our image, after our likeness: and let them have dominion over the fish of the sea, and over the fowl of the air, and over all the cattle, and over every creeping thing that creepth upon the earth." Readers take a moment and read Genesis 1-3 chapters along with this book. Remember what you read in the second chapter of this book, "Lucifer, first ruler, of the Earth" he was tested and he failed his test.

Adam, the second ruler, of the recreated earth was given dominion over everything in this earth. He wasn't just given dominion in the Garden of Eden, but over everything in the earth.

God made Adam and Eve free mortal agents. He didn't make them robots, but He gave them the power of choice. Deuteronomy 30:19 KJV "I call heaven and earth to record this day against you, that I have set before you, life and death, blessing and cursing: therefore choose life that both thou and thy seed may live."

Adam was given instructions how to walk with his Creator that he and his wife would be blessed. Adam was given a simple test, and he was to obey his Creator that he might live in complete harmony with Him.

Genesis 2:16-17 verses KJV "And the LORD God commanded the man saying, of every tree of the garden thou mayest freely eat: But of the tree of knowledge of good and evil, thou shalt not eat of it: for in the day that thou eatest thereof thou shalt surely die." Adam felled his test and caused chaos in the earth.

Sin entered into the earth because of one man's sin. Adam was the "Representative of the Human Race." (KJV-Romans 5:12) This recreated earth was in chaos because sin had entered into it because of one man's disobedience. Even the whole creature groaned and travails in pain together until now, because of the curse that is upon the earth. Even we Christians groan within ourselves, waiting for the adoption to wit, the redemption of our bodies. (KJV-Romans 8:19-23)

Adam was born-again from life unto death. He died spiritually that same day when he disobeyed God. Spiritual death is separation from our Creator, God! I don't know how long Adam walked with God before he chose to disobey, but he lost both his relationship and, the fellowship that he had with Him in the beginning. Adam, the "Branch", was disconnected from God, the "True Vine." (KJV-John 15:1-5) Have you ever wondered how mankind lost his way from serving the only true and living God? We have lost our way and connection with God because of sin.

This is the purpose that Jesus came to the earth to declare our Creator to us, and to reconcile us back to God. II Corinthians 5:19 KJV says, " To wit, that God was in Christ, reconciling the world unto himself, not imputing their trespasses unto them; and hath committed unto us the word of reconciliation." I will write more about this in the last chapter of this book.

Adam was separated from God when he disobeyed. There is a difference in the first Adam and men that was born after Adam. First, Adam was the only man God created. We came through the seed of Adam. (Genesis 1:28)

God breathe into Adam the breath of life and he became a living "Soul." (KJV-Genesis 2:7) The law of the Spirit of life and peace reigns in Adam's mortal body because the Spirit of God dwelt in him. (KJV-Romans 8:2)

When Adam disobeyed God the law of sin and death began to reign in his spirit the day he sinned. Romans 8:2 KJV says, "For the law of the Spirit of life in Christ Jesus hath made me free from the law of sin and death."

Adam died the same day he disobeyed God. He died spiritually. This is called "Spiritual death which means separation from God.

C.I. Scofield, D. D. says, in his New Scofield Study Bible that "Spiritual Death" is the state of the natural or unregenerate person as still in his sin, alienated from the life of God, and destitute of the Spirit. (Ephesians 2:5; 4:18, 19; Romans 8:9) All men died in Adam, and inherit his sinful nature. I Corinthians 15:22 KJV says, "For as in Adam all die even so in Christ shall all be made alive."

The moment we are born we began to die because of the law of the spirit of sin and death that reigns in our mortal bodies.

If "Spiritual Death" is prolonged beyond the death of the body, spiritual death becomes eternal separation from God in conscious suffering. This is called the "Second Death." (Revelation 2:11) This is why Jesus told Nicodemus with urgency: "Ye must be born-again." The sinner man is still a triune being made in the image of God, but he is dead in his trespasses and sin.

The Spirit of God in the sinner is quickened when he hears the word of God, and he becomes a new creature after he accepts Jesus as his personal Savior.

Paul, the Apostle, says, "And you hath he quickened, who were dead in trespasses and sins; Wherein in times past ye walked according to the prince of this world, according to the power of the air, the spirit that now worketh in the children of disobedience."

"Even when we were dead in sins, hath quickened us together with Christ (by grace are ye saved;) And hath raised us up together, and made us sit together in heavenly places in Christ Jesus." (KJV-Ephesians 2:1-2,5-6)

God quickened His Spirit in me when I heard the word of God, but I didn't become a new creature until I accepted Jesus as my Savior and Lord. When I accepted Jesus as my Savior the Spirit of God came into my spirit, and now the law of life and peace reigns in me, instead of the law of sin and death. (KJV-Romans 8:2,11)

Adam was born-again from life unto death. Adam was the first "Backslider."

"Backslider" is a term that is used today when a Christian throws in the towel and backs up instead of going forward in God. Thank God he forgave Adam and his wife, Eve. Genesis 3:21 KJV "Unto Adam also and to his wife did the LORD God make coats of skins, and clothed them."

Fig leaves could not save Adam and Eve, but the blood sacrifice of an animal had to be shed to atone for their sins.

Reader, only God can clothe us in righteousness through the blood of Jesus who gave his life as a ransom for many. (KJV-Mark 10:45) Hebrews 9:22 KJV "And almost all things are by the law purged with blood; and without shedding of blood is no remission."

Like all backsliders who are filled with the Spirit of God they have to be restored back to God. The Spirit of God didn't die in Adam nor did he have a dead spirit. God is life and His Spirit doesn't die. When Adam disobeyed God sin and death reigned in Adam's spirit instead of life, and God couldn't quickened His Spirit in Adam because he chose to separate himself from his Creator. (KJV-Romans 8:2,11)

Adam died the same day he disobeyed God. Genesis 2:17 KJV says, "But of the tree of the knowledge of good and evil, thou shalt not eat of it: for in the day that thou eatest thereof thou shalt surely die." He was disconnected, detached, from Almighty God his only source of life until God in His love and mercy forgave him through the shed blood of an animal sacrifice. (Genesis 2:21) This was temporary until Jesus could come on the scene and become the ultimate sacrifice.

When the sinner comes to God through His Son, Jesus, and asks God for forgiveness of their sin they are born-again from death unto life. Jesus quickens the sinner' spirit by the word of God, and if he accepts Jesus he becomes a new creature. John 5:21 KJV "For as the Father raiseth up the dead, and quickeneth them even so the Son quickeneth whom he will."

The sinner has a choice when he hears the word of God when God quickens His Spirit in him to either accept or reject Jesus. II Corinthians 15:45 KJV says, "And so it written, The first man Adam was made a living soul; the last Adam was made a quickening spirit." To all those who say they will come to God when they get ready the latter part of that verse says, "The Son quickeneth whom he will."(KJV- John 5:21) We must understand we are not in control of anything and God is in control of everything even our lives. John 6:44 KJV "No man can come to me, except the Father which hath sent me draw him: and I will raise him up at the last day."

Genesis 2:7 KJV "And the Lord God formed man of the dust of the ground, and breathe into his nostrils the breath of life; and man became a living soul."

Jesus breathed on his disciples and they received the Holy Ghost after his resurrection before the day of Pentecost. (KJV-John 20:22)

When Adam sinned he died that same day spiritually. Adam was made in the image of God after his likeness, and so is the sinner for everything follows after his own kind. Spiritual death is separation from God. All died in the first Adam. (Romans 5:12;I Corinthians 15:22) Let's look at the word "Separation."

Let me give you an example of what the word separation means: Jack becomes unfaithful to his wife, Susan, and moves to another state and has no contact or relationship with her. Jack has broken the "Marriage Covenant", but neither Jack nor Susan has filed for divorce. This is what we call "Separation." They are not married they are separated. Marriage is two people living under the same roof and operating within the laws of Matrimony according to the word of God.

This couple can only talk about their pass relationship. Jack and Susan's marriage is going through a state of what we call "Loose Ends." The definition of "Loose Ends" is "Unfinished Business." Legally they will not be able to marry again or buy property separate from the other because the law of Matrimony binds them together.

Reader there is no "Loose Ends" in God. God made a Covenant with Adam, the "Edenic Covenant" and Adam broke his part of the agreement. God sought Adam in the garden and dealt with Adam's sin.

Genesis 3:9 KJV says, "And the Lord God called unto Adam, and said unto him, Where art Thou?" Reader sin has to be dealt with and we must become responsible for our actions. God dealt with all parties involved. My theory about Eve: She could have eaten all the fruit of the Tree of knowledge of Good and Evil and nothing would have changed because Adam was the Representative of the Human Race. Jesus, is called the last Adam, (KJV-I Corinthians 15:45) and He became the representative of the Human race.

He came to undo what the first Adam did through His Life, Death, Burial, and Resurrection. Romans 5:17 KJV "For if by one man's offence death reigned by one; much more they which receive abundance of grace and of the gift of righteousness shall reign in life by one, Jesus Christ."

If Adam had eaten from the Tree of Life after he had partook of the "Tree of knowledge of good and evil he would have lived forever in that sinful state. God in His infinite wisdom and mercy drove Adam out of the garden. (KJV-Genesis 3:22-24)

God made provision for Adam to fellowship with him in a new way through the blood sacrifice of animals and he received forgiveness of his sins. (KJV-Genesis 3:21)

Adam didn't forget his experiences and knowledge he had of his Creator before he sinned. Adam had the life of God in him before he sinned. The sinner doesn't have the knowledge of God because he is born in sin. Some religions profess to know the word of God, and haven't accepted Jesus as their personal Savior.

They try to study and teach the scriptures without the Spirit of God and they quote the letter of the word. Second Corinthians 3:6 KJV "Who also hath made us able, ministers of the new testament; not of the letter, but of the spirit: for the letter killeth, but the spirit giveth life." The word of God is spiritually discerned. (KJV-I Corinthians 2:14) God hadn't given Adam any grounds to separate or divorce him for He was faithfully. Adam chose to separate from his Creator, God, and made a Covenant with sin and death when he obeyed Satan instead of God. When Adam chose this course of action he died that same day spiritually.

John 6:63 KJV "It is the spirit that quickeneth, the flesh profiteth nothing: the words that I speak unto you, they are spirit, and they are life." The "eth" in quickeneth means continuation. God didn't quicken Adam's spirit because he is now separated from Him because of sin. Believer you must continue to live a godly life before God so He can continue to quicken your mortal body. (KJV- Romans 8:11)
The sinner may hear the word of God over and over through preaching, or witnessing, but the word of God is what quickens the Spirit of God in him and when this happens he has the opportunity to accept Jesus or reject Him.

How can they call on him in whom they have not believed? This is why we must witness that souls may be won to Christ. Every one of us have the "Ministry of Reconciliation." (Romans10: 14,15; II Corinthians 5:17) Hearing the word of God ignites our faith, and quickeneth the Spirit of God in the believer and also quickens the spirit in the sinner through His word to draw him to Christ.
Romans 10:17 KJV says, "So then faith cometh by hearing, and hearing by the word of God." Every man has a measure of faith. (KJV-Romans 12:3) When we accept Christ as our Lord and Savior the Spirit of God comes into our spirit and we become a new creature. (KJV-II Corinthians 5:17) Romans 8:9 KJV says, "But ye are not in the flesh, but in the Spirit, if so be that the Spirit of God dwell in you. Now if any man have not the Spirit of Christ, he is none of his."

Backsliding doesn't happen overnight it's a process. Same token learning about our Creator is also a process.
Isaiah 28:10 KJV "For precept must be upon precept, precept upon precept; line upon line, line upon line; here a little, and there a little." Christ quickens His Spirit in the backslider when he hears the word of God. This is why Satan tries to isolate him from hearing God's word.   It doesn't tell us how long Adam walked

24

with his Creator before he disobeyed. Adam had a lot to tell his family about God for he had a relationship with Him before he sinned. God's will is to restore mankind back to the place of fellowship through His Son, Jesus.

Man that was born after Adam served God through offering the blood of animals as a sacrifice unto God by faith for the forgiveness of sin. (KJV-Hebrews 9:22) The Spirit of God came upon a select few: Kings, Prophets, Priests, and Judges. The "Soul" made men self-conscious. The body houses both the Soul and the Spirit and the Body makes men world conscious. Sin made men's heart hard, and he turned away from God his only source of life.

Praise God, God promised through the prophet, Ezekiel, that He would put His Spirit in our temple, that we can keep and walk in his Statues, Ordinances and Laws.

Ezekiel 36:26 KJV "A new heart also will I give you, and a new spirit will I put within you: and I will take away the stony heart out of your flesh, and I will give you an heart of flesh. 27 And I will put my spirit within you, and cause you to walk in my statues, and ye shall keep my judgments, and do them.." God fulfilled his promise in the New Testament through his Son, Jesus. (Matthew 3:11;Acts 1:8; 2:4)

Does this statement sound familiar? "I'm not hurting anybody, but myself." We must remember when we yield our wills to sin against God it will affect our lives and cause others' lives to be effected. Adam and Eve lost two sons in one day because of their disobedience. They lost many things when they disobeyed God. There are consequences in every wrong choice we make and the price is costly. It costs too much to sin, for the wages of sin is death. (KJV-Romans 6:23)

Reader do not despair there is yet hope for man through His Son, Christ, Jesus. He paid the price for our sins and his blood washes our sins away. Not just our past sins, but both present and future sins.

I John 1:7 KJV says, "But if we walk in the light, we have fellowship one with another, and the blood of Jesus Christ his Son cleanseth us from all sins." Christian, we don't practice sin, but if we sin we have an advocate with the Father, Jesus Christ the righteous. (KJV-I John 2:1)

Stop a moment and meditate on what you have read thus far, and take inventory of your life. Ask yourself a question; "Are you a Born-again, Christian, or are you separated from God because of sin? (KJV-Isaiah 59:1,2)

Adam was Born-again from life unto death, but God in His mercy killed an animal and shed its' blood and clothed them in righteousness. (KJV-Genesis 3:21) Romans 3:23 KJV says, "For all have sinned, and come short of the glory of God." Jesus paid our sin debt, and it's our responsibility to accept His sacrifice.

I Thessalonians 5:23 KJV "And the very God of peace sanctify you wholly; and I pray God your whole spirit and soul and body be preserved blameless unto the coming of our LORD Jesus Christ."

Go back to chapter one and read it over until you get the understanding that you are made in the image of God. Christians the born-again man he is triune: Spirit, Soul, and Body. (KJV- I Thessalonians 5:23) This is why Jesus told Nicodemus "Ye must be born-again."(KJV-John 3:3,7)

Chapter 5
Regenerate Man

Webster's dictionary says regenerate means to reform spiritually or morally. 2. To form, construct, or create anew. We will find this word in the King James Version in the book of Titus. Titus 3:4,5 KJV "But after that the kindness and love of God our Savior toward man appeared, 5 Not by works of righteousness which we have done, but by the washing of regeneration, and renewing of the Holy Ghost." Take your time and read Titus 3:1-11 this is the only book of the Bible that has the word "Regeneration."

II Corinthians 5:17 KJV "Therefore if any man be in Christ, he is a new creature: old things are passed away; behold, all things are become new." Although the word regeneration is found only in the book of Titus, Paul, the Apostle, began to write to the Corinthians Church these two words "New Creature." He told them they were new creatures that old things had passed away and behold all things had become new. The word "Regeneration" means the same as "New Creature" or create anew. Jesus told Nicodemus "Ye must be born-again." (KJV-John 3:3,7) All men died in Adam because of sin, and this is why all men must be born-again. (Romans 5:12) Regeneration connects men back to their Creator and he regains what the first Adam lost through our Lord, and Savior, Jesus Christ. "Something we have to do" is what every believer and unbeliever must understand. Christ died for every man and they must accept Him as the only sacrifice for their sin. They can't earn Salvation through works but by grace are we saved. (KJV-Ephesians 2:5-9) We must yield our will totally to God even after we pray, fast, and study His word. The "Will" is very powerful that God has given men through his soul. Look what God says in Genesis concerning the power of the Soul.

Genesis 11:6 KJV "And the LORD said, Behold, the people is one, and they have all one language; and this they begin to do: and now nothing will be restrained from them, which they have imagined to do."

The people decided to build them a tower whose top would reach unto the heaven. Take a moment and read Genesis 11:1-9th verses. Notice God, didn't say it couldn't be done on the contrary He said the people have all one language, and this they begin to do, and nothing would be restrained from them which they have imagined.

Imaginations come through the soul nature, and people have seen images in their mind's eye the things they have desired to accomplish. Then through the act of the will they set out to do the things they image in their minds, and didn't stop until it came into manifestation. A good example is a person desiring a new car and the craving for that car can become so strong that their sense of smell can literally smell the leather, the newness, of the vehicle. They might have been in someone's new car or went to test drive one lately.

The sense of smell kicks in because of the desire for that automobile through the soul nature. It makes no difference whether they have the finance at this time or not, but as they see themselves driving the car they will work toward their goal and set their sights on fulfilling everything they have imagined in their mind.

II Corinthians 10:4,5 KJV "For the weapons of our warfare are not carnal, but mighty through God to pulling down of strong hold; 5 Casting down imaginations, and every high thing that exalteth itself against the knowledge of God, and bringing into captivity every thought to obedience of Christ."

All imaginations are not evil. The Wright brothers built the airplane; first it began as an image they saw in their mind's eye before the actual manifestation of their aircraft was built, and came into existence in the natural realm. Reader the spiritual realm is just as real as the natural realm. Many men and women have accomplished great things through their imaginations that come from their soul even after sin entered the earth.

Genesis 6:5 KJV "And God saw that the wickedness of man was great in the earth, and that every imagination of the thoughts of his heart was only evil continually." When the LORD saw that men decided to build a city and a tower whose top may reach unto heaven; and was planning to have one name, stay in one place, and become one race the God-Head went into council and agreed together to confound their language. (Genesis 11:1-9)

We must submit ourselves totally to God and let Him have preeminence, and renew our mind daily with the word of God. (KJV-Romans 12:1,2)

Remember Lucifer, and Adam was not omniscient. Christians, we must understand that even though the Spirit of God dwells in our mortal bodies we still don't know everything.

Paul said it like this: Acts 17:28 KJV "For in him we live, and move, and have our being; as certain also of your own poets have said, For we are also his offspring.

The important thing to remember is as God gives us delegated authority we must obey, and walk in complete harmony with them. God is the "Potter" and we are the "Clay."(KJV-Jeremiah 18:1-6)

We are just stewards over our Children, Congregation, and whatever God has given into our charge. So we must stay humble before God and not get lifted up in pride like Lucifer, and Adam who both disobey the word of God.

We have His word, and His Spirit abides in us, but we are yet learning about our Heavenly Father through the things we suffer. The scriptures teach about Him and others who either obeyed or disobeyed so we want walk down the wrong path. (KJV- I Corinthians 10:6)

Reasoning (imaginations) comes through our soul nature and God wants us to use it for His glory. This is why the thought life is very important. Paul, the Apostle, through the inspiration of the Spirit tells us what we should mediate on.

"Finally, brethren, whatsoever things are true, whatsoever things are honest, whatsoever things are just, whatsoever things are pure, whatsoever things are of good report; if there be any virtue, and if there be any praise, think on these things." (KJV-Philippians 4:8)

"Now that we have accepted Christ, Jesus, as our personal Savior, our mind must be reprogrammed through the word of God. (KJV-Romans 12:1,2) When Adam sinned his "Soul" controlled his "Body" and led it selfishly down the wrong path. Don't forget the "Spirit" causes man to be God-Conscious, and the "Soul" causes man to be self-conscious. The soul thinks only of itself what it can gain or profit from someone or something. Yielding our wills to the Spirit of God will cause us to be victorious Christians. Even when we pray, fast, study His word, and attend Church services regularly this is not enough it's only the beginning.

For if we don't yield our wills totally to God we will be defeated Christians. You might ask: "How do I yield my will totally to God? We yield to the Spirit of God by giving him the right away in our lives through obeying His word.

If we don't let God set on the throne of our hearts we will be what Paul calls a carnal-minded Christian. Romans 8:5 KJV says, "For they that are after the flesh do mind the things of the flesh; but they that are after the Spirit the things of the Spirit. 6 For to be carnally minded is death, but to be spiritual minded is life and peace."

James put it this way; James 1:22 KJV "But be ye doers of the word, and not hearers only, deceiving your own selves." (Read James 1:21-25) Many great men and women of God have missed out on God because they simply didn't yield their wills to God. They sought God for all the wrong reasons to gain the anointing so they could minister to others, but they didn't yield their wills to God. They began to preach to others and became a castaway. (KJV-I Corinthians 9:27) Let's take a look at one of the twelve Apostles "Judas Iscariot", an Apostle, of Jesus Christ. He walked with Jesus and saw the miracles that Jesus performed.
He also heard the word of God. Jesus gave him power along with the others to preach, teach, heal, and cast out devils in His name.

(KJV-Matthew 10:1-4)   Yet Judas betrayed his Lord, and Savior, Christ Jesus.

Many say that Judas didn't have a choice for it was written in the book of Psalms that a friend would betray Christ. Psalm 41:9 KJV "Yea mine own familiar friend, in whom I trusted, which did eat of my bread, hath lifted up his heel against me."
Reader, my God is a just God, He gives everyone a chance to choose life or death, blessing or cursing. In Deuteronomy 30:19 God tells us to choose life that our seed and we might live. (KJV) Judas was tested like all the others, but he failed his test. He heard Jesus say, "For what is a man profited, if he shall gain the whole world, and lose his own soul? Or what shall a man give in exchange for his soul?" (KJV-Matthew 16:26)

Yet Judas Iscariot chose the way of unrighteousness. Satan caused him to hang himself and he failed headlong and his bowels gushed out. (KJV-Acts 1:18)
That's what Satan wants to do to "Christians." When we yield our wills totally to Satan he comes to steal, kill and destroy our souls. (John 10:10)   Satan has set his sights on man to cause him to reject God's word so he may obtain spiritual death, separation from God, instead of eternal life.

Our Father promises us both abundant and eternal life through Christ Jesus. (John 10:10)   Isaiah 1:19,20 KJV "If ye be willing and obedient, ye shall eat the good of the land: 20 But if ye refuse and rebel, ye shall be devoured with the sword: for the mouth of the Lord hath spoken it."

Now that we are "New Creatures" we must choose life and the blessing through obedience to God's word. Reader, remember God will never tell you to obey his word without given you the power through the Holy Ghost to perform His every command. He never gives us a test without giving us the answers to that test which is in the word of God.

Chapter 6
The Ball is in your Court

I pray that you are beginning to understand what the will of God is for your life. His plan and purpose for your life has already been set in motion. Even though this statement is true you are still the one who will play an important role that will determine your destiny that God has for you. Has anyone ever told you you'll never amount to anything? What about friends, family, and enemies who say you never reach your goals?

Let's look at Joseph my favorite young man. God's destination for Joseph was to send him to Egypt and raise him up in the midst of the famine to saved His chosen nation, Israel. Take time to read Genesis 37-50 chapters.

Joseph, was a Covenant man, of God. He trusted in the God of Israel in whom his forefathers, and father, Israel served.

Joseph, a young man, who loved God lived a godly life, but suffered persecution from his own brethren. II Timothy 3:12 KJV says, "Yea, and all that will live godly in Christ Jesus shall suffer persecution." His brethren were jealous because of the love that their father had for Joseph. God began to reveal to Joseph in a dream His plan for his life. He was so excited about the dream he told his father and brethren. It was already done in the mind of God to bring his people out of the famine and make them a great nation before he called Joseph to this great task. Romans 4:17-KJV ("As it is written, I have made thee a father of many nations,) before him whom he believed, even God, who quickeneth the dead, and calleth those things which be not as though they were. "

When God reveals His plan to us He is showing us the end result. Many times we don't see the beginning or the middle, but he shows us the end because in the mind of God its' already done.

Let's move on to see how God plans to get Joseph to Egypt. Reader, God is in control of your life just like He was in control of Joseph's life. The word of God says they hated him the more for his dream. Jealous turned into hatred and soon hatred turned into murder. They plotted to kill Joseph, but God intervened in his life. They sold him into slavery for twenty-pieces of silver to the Midianites, and the Midianites sold him unto Potiphar, Captain, of the guard in Egypt. (KJV-Genesis 38:28:39:1) Joseph's brethren was also in the will of God, they got Joseph a free ticket to Egypt. God will use us as a vessel of honor or a vessel of dishonor as he used his brethren. (KJV-Romans 9:21)

Let me bring you up to date before we get into the story about Joseph and tell you a little concerning his great-grandfather Abraham. In the Dispensation of Promise, men serve God by faith through the act of their will (Soul). Since Adam, the father was Priest, in the home he offered unto God animal sacrifices for his sin, and his family. (Hebrews 9:26,27) God then took him out a people from Abraham's seed, which became the nation of Israel. Joseph was the great-grandson of Abraham before Israel became a nation. God was preserving His people so that His promise to Abraham to make his seed a great nation would be fulfilled. All of this is part of our Salvation even the gift of the Holy Ghost. Abraham didn't have an inkling of what God was going to do for both Jews and Gentiles. Abraham was a Gentile. I said earlier the Spirit of God came upon a select few, but today we have the Holy Ghost dwelling on the inside. First Corinthians 6:19 KJV says, "What? Know ye not that your body is the temple of the Holy Ghost which is in you, which ye have of God, and ye are not your own." Adam had the Spirit of God inside his temple and he had the power to keep God's statues and judgments. He had the power within him to pass his test, but he chose to disobey. (I Timothy 2:13-14) Contrary to popular beliefs Eve didn't caused Adam to disobey God this is erroneous doctrine. Adam willingly sinned.

This scripture revealed that God gave Adam delegated authority as the head of his family and dominion over everything in the Earth. He had God's instructions concerning the "Tree of

Knowledge of Good and Evil", and the consequences it would bring upon him if he disobeyed. It was Adam's responsibility to protect and provide for his family. Earlier in the book I said I believe if Eve had eaten all the fruit that was on the "Tree of knowledge of Good and Evil" nothing would have changed because Adam was the representative of the "Human Race." Satan through the serpent knew this so he used Eve to get to her husband, Adam, but he still had a choice to obey or disobey.

Adam chose to disobey God, and blamed his Creator for his action. Genesis 3:12 KJV" And the man said, the woman whom thou gravest to be with me, she gave me of the tree and I did eat."

This is an example of the soul lusting against the spirit. Galatians 5:16-17 KJV says, "This I say then, Walk in the Spirit, and ye shall not fulfill the lust of the flesh. For the flesh lusteth against the Spirit 17 and the Spirit against flesh: and these are contrary the one to the other: so that ye cannot do the things that ye would." Just a note to women, the little Eves', God has given us an influencing spirit as help meets to help our husbands fulfill their destiny. We must not use this gift the wrong way as Eve did, but use it for the glory and honor of God. We as individuals are responsible for the choices we make and the actions that we take. When question by God, Eve blamed the serpent. (KJV- Genesis 3:13)   I believe that if the serpent had known what hit it, it would have blamed Satan, but God didn't ask the serpent. Adam wasn't omniscience like God and he didn't know about Satan, the falling angel, but God gave him all the information that he needed to use his delegated authority over every creature. (Genesis 1:26)   In other words Adam was told to subdue anything that got out of line with the word of God, and he was to stay in complete harmony with his Creator. (Genesis 1:28)

Instead he just stood there and let Satan steal, kill, and destroy his happy home. (John 10:10)   This is the reason Jesus told Nicodemus; "Ye must be born-again" to gain the victory over Satan through his Son, Jesus. (John 3:3,7)

Genesis 6:5 KJV "And God saw that the wickedness of man was great in the earth, and that every imagination of the thoughts of his heart was only evil continually." The word "Heart" here is the same as the "Soul" in this scripture. For the imagination (reasoning) and thought life comes from the soul nature.

We have a better Covenant established upon better promises in the Dispensation of Grace and Truth. (Hebrews 8:6) Thank God, Jesus was the ultimate sacrifice for mankind's sin once and for all. (Hebrews 10:7-14) The Born-again man can serve God in Spirit and in Truth. (KJV-John 4:23,24)

This is the promise that God gave to Ezekiel that he would put His Spirit within us and it has been fulfilled in this dispensation of "Grace and Truth." He has put His Spirit in our temple, and we can keep His statues and judgements. (Ezekiel 36:26,27; Acts 1:8; 2:17,18)

Just what does this statement mean "The ball is in your Court?" We read that Joseph has been sold into Egypt by the Midanites to Potiphar, Captain, of the Guard. We taught earlier in this book about the importance of choices that we make or made, and how it will affect everyone around us. Every human being must become accountable for their actions. (KJV-Deuteronomy 30:19)

Now let's examine the statement "The ball is in your Court." God has given Joseph a dream and has revealed only the end result of His dream. Yet he doesn't fully understand it, but one thing Joseph knew that God was in control of his life. Joseph, a Covenant man of God, has been sold to the highest bidder for the price of a slave.

Let's look at this seventeen-year old boy's life just for a moment. His own brethren have rejected him, and he has been sold into slavery for twenty pieces of silver. He has been seduced by his owner's wife and thrown in jail because of her false accusation. Now what will Joseph do?

Will he trust God or will he blame God for all his trials and tribulations. The ball is in his Court. Joseph had every right to be bitter in man's eyes, but not God's.

He had a choice to give up on God, and say what's the use if it's not one thing it's another. God, knew He, could depend on Joseph passing every test, and he came out smelling like a sweet smelling savor.

In the process of time Joseph understood that God had been preparing him to become Governor of the land to save His people from the famine. (KJV-Genesis 45:8) When Israel, Joseph's father, died his guilty, and fearful brothers sent a messenger to him saying our father said forgive our trespass, and they offer themselves servants unto Joseph. (Genesis 50:15-21) Joseph chose to serve God even in the midst of fiery trials, and he chose to forgive his brethren.

Joseph had both the opportunity, and authority to destroy his brethren and reject the God of Israel, but instead he made the right choice. The ball was in Joseph's court, and he played ball wisely. We must choose wisely, and be merciful to others, as God has been to us.

A word of advice to counselors in whatever position God has called you unto; never let an individual trap you into making a decision for them. The moment something happens they will blame you. We can give people the information they need from the word of God and our experience, but they must make their own choices. Never make an individual feel guilty for choosing what they thought was best for them. This is what this statement means, "The Ball is in your Court." Many times people will say you didn't listen to me or take my advice this is why things didn't work out for you. This might be true or false, and we know that in Adam's case God knew what was best for him. Yet God didn't override Adam's "Will."

He knew that the recreated Earth and mankind would be in chaos when Adam disobeyed. He also knew the choice he would make. We will talk more about this in the last chapter of this book. Yet God who is omnipotent allows man to choose his destiny. (Deuteronomy 30:19) When we impose our "Will" on someone else this becomes nothing but a thin veil of "Witchcraft."

Did you know a person has a right to choose to go to Heaven and hold on to your hat, and a right to choose to go to Hell? (Deuteronomy 30:19)   Don't misunderstand what I'm saying through the power of the Holy Ghost. We must establish authority in our homes, schools, and churches. Authority must be established in the Earth. We must give the needed information and we must tell them the consequences if the rules or not followed. Then like God we step back and allow them to choose. Reader we must stop blaming others for the position or place we are in today. We are there because of the choices we made.

Let's ask ourselves a question; Are we greater than our Creator? God gives men free choice. He is a free mortal agent. God gave Adam a simple commandment so he could prove whether he would be loyal and faithful to Him. The beginning part of Genesis 2:17 KJV says, 'But of the tree of the knowledge of good and evil, thou shalt not eat of it." That scripture in Genesis 2:17 was the commandment and the consequences of disobeying its' command was death. Latter part of Genesis 2:17 KJV says, "for in the day that thou eatest thereof thou shalt surely die."

God didn't make that decision for Adam he simply gave him all the information that he needed, and then He gave him the ability (power) to obey. God gives men the power of choice and He gives them the ability to obey the word through His Son, Jesus Christ. Even though God knows what's best for us He will not override our Wills. Proverbs 22:6 says "Train up a child in the way he should go: and when he is old, he will not depart from it." Parents never worry about the choices your children will make or made, because if you trained them as Proverbs 22:6 KJV said you can rest and give them to God. He called us as good stewards (Parents) not to make their decision only to teach and train them in the way they should go. (Proverbs 22:6; Ephesians 6:4)

Don't forget "God is in Control." I believe this statement gave both men and women of God strength down through the ages. It helped men like Joseph to endure their hardships as a good solider, and fulfill his destiny that God had set for him. It took our Lord and Savior all the way to the cross.

When we make decisions for others we take from them their power of choice, and we override their will. We can't live other people lives. We can only live our own lives and as the song writer put it, "One day at a time sweet Jesus." This is what the statement means "The Ball is in Your Court." It's up to the individual to choose life or death, blessing or cursing that thou and thou seed shall live. (KJV-Deuteronomy 30:19)

Chapter 7
Why so many Christians Backslide

Backsliding is a term used in the Christian language to describe a person that has falling from Grace. Adam was the first "Backslider" who was born-again from life unto death.

Hebrews 6:6 "If they shall fall away, to renew them again unto repentance; seeing they crucify to themselves the Son of God afresh, and put him to an open shame."

Throwing in the towel is an expression that we use when a person gives up the will to fight. There is that word "Will" again, we must understand God is not going to do anything more than what He has already done through His Son, Jesus. Christians will say, "I'm waiting on God" to move or do something about this situation. Here is an eye opening, God is waiting on you to believe and obey His word.

Backsliding is taking you backwards instead of forward from everything you were taught, and leading you down the wrong path to serve Satan, who are God and Man's enemy. (KJV-Hebrews 6:4-5) Reader if you are a backslider cheer up for the Gospel of Jesus Christ is good news. God is married to the backslider. Jeremiah 3:14 KJV "Turn, O backsliding children, saith the Lord; for I am married unto you: and I will take you one of a city, and two of a family, and I will bring you to Zion.

Walking with the Lord every day for twenty-six years wasn't always easy or shall I say everyday wasn't Sunday. How do we purpose in our hearts to live for Jesus especially when all hell seems to break loose in our lives? We live for the Lord one day at a time. We must yield our wills totally to God no matter what the situation appears or feels like.

Paul, the Apostle, wrote to the Roman Church: "For therein is the righteousness of God revealed from faith to faith: as it is written, the just shall live by faith." (Romans 1:17) "For we walk by faith, not by sight." (II Corinthians 5:7)

The will is powerful, and as we yield our will totally to God we can accomplish anything through faith in Him. Paul says, "I can do all things through Christ, which strengtheneth me. (Philippians 4:13) We can't make excuses why we are not strong in Him because God has given us everything that pertaineth to life and godliness. (II Peter 1:3-7) Many Saints make excuses why they continue to live a defeated life, and to justify their sins they confess; "I'm not strong as others." Paul says, "There hath no temptation taken you but such is common to man: but God is faithful, who will not suffer you to be tempted above that ye are able; but will with the temptation also make a way to escape, that ye may be able to bear it." (I Corinthians 10:13)

Haven't you heard a doctor say to one family member that their father doesn't have any more fight in him or the will to live and to another family your mother has a strong will and she is fighting this disease? We are Spirit, Soul, and Body made in the image of God. When we yield our wills totally to God we are yielding our wills to the Spirit. We are allowing the Spirit to be in controlled of our lives. We can't allow the Soul to dictate to the body the path it should take or walk. Paul talks about the war between the two natures in Romans the seventh chapter reader, read that whole chapter.

"For that which I do I allow not: for what I would, that do I not; but what I hate, that do I." (Romans 7:15) The Soul had the preeminence over our bodies a long time that Paul had to confess, even after he was born-again about the struggle he was having concerning these two natures.

His sinful nature that dwelled in him before his conversion, and the godly nature that made him a new creature. He had to gain victory over his sinful habits that he brought with him when he came to Christ Jesus. He had to get rid of old baggage.

Then praise God in the eight chapter of Romans Paul says, "There is therefore now no condemnation to them which are in Christ Jesus, who walk not after the flesh, but after the Spirit." (KJV-Romans 8:1) Christians, we must yield our will totally to God by choosing to walk after the Spirit as an act of our will, and

40

not fulfill the lust of the flesh. The Soul doesn't have the power to override the Spirit. What we are feeling comes through the Soul nature, and that desire or appetite can cause us to believe it is in control of our life.

Remember God is in control of your life, but we must make the right choice. Will we walk in what we feel in our emotions, or choose to stand on the word of God? Paul calls it the "Flesh." Satan will also make you believe that he is still in control of your life, but John says in I John 4:4 KJV "Ye are of God, little children, and have overcome them: because greater is he that is in you, than he that is in the world. If you are not filled with the Spirit of God asked God to fill you now. The Holy Ghost, He, is a gift, from God.

Backslider, don't let the devil tell you it's too late and that you have missed God. From the time we ask God to forgive us of our sin until the day we go home to be with the Lord the blood of Jesus continues to wash away our sin. (KJV-I John 1:7) "If we confess our sins, he is faithful and just to forgive us our sins, and to cleanse us from all unrighteousness." (KJV-I John 1:9) We don't practice sin, but if we sin John, the Apostle, says in I John 2:2 "My little children, these things write I unto you, that ye sin not. And if any man sin, we have an advocate with the Father, Jesus Christ the righteous."

We must yield our will totally to God in this Christian walk. Salvation is our life, and we are preparing ourselves for eternity. Only what we do for Christ will last. When driving our cars we yield to the yield sign, which gives the other driver the right away. When we yield our wills totally to God we give him the right away to sit on the throne of our hearts. We are not in control of our lives, for we have been bought with a price, and we are not our own. (KJV-I Corinthians 6:19,20)

This book is written to Christians, backsliders and sinners everywhere to exhort you to know that God loves you. We want you to know we (Christians) are not perfect (mature), but we are forgiven. Paul put it this way: "Not as though I had already attained, either were already perfect: but I follow after, if that I may apprehend that for which also I am apprehended of Christ Jesus. (Philippians 3:12)

Paul, the Apostle, considered himself to be a chief sinner, before he accepted Christ as his Savior. He did many horrible things in his life before salvation, but he said he was forgetting those things, which were behind him, and was pressing toward the mark for the prize of the high calling of God in Christ Jesus. (KJV-Philippians 3:13,14) Paul, the Apostle, was yielding his will totally to God no matter what bad memories he had of his pass life. He knew he was forgiven and he decided to forget and forgive himself and put the past behind him.

Don't just seek God for His anointing, and the ministry gift in your life, but seek to know Him. Paul, the Apostle, said it this way: "That I may know him, and the power of his resurrection, and the fellowship of his sufferings, being made conformable unto his death; If by any means I might attain unto the resurrection of the dead." (KJV-Philippians 3:10-11) For we don't want to preach or witness to others and become a castaway. (KJV- I Corinthians 9:27)

Chapter 8
Choose ye this Day

I Kings 18:21 "And Elijah came unto all the people, and said, How long halt ye between two opinions? If the Lord be God, follow him: but if Baal, then follow him. And the people answered him not a word."

Notice in this scripture Elijah, the Prophet, gave the people a choice, when he said if the Lord be God, follow him, but if Baal then follow him. Elijah knew that people were free mortal agents and they had the power of choice.

Here's a rule of thumb to go by when you counseling never allow anyone to put you into a position to make their decision even though you see the choices they are making will hurt them in the long run. Let's learn an important lesson from this passage of scriptures concerning Elijah, the Prophet, and God's people. He gave them the word of the Lord and he let them choose whom they would serve God or Baal. Never use your delegated authority that you received from God to override another person's will. When you override another person's will this is operating in the "spirit of Witchcraft." Watch out this will cause a person to become co-dependent, and they will start trusting in you instead of God.

God has made men free mortal agents. He has given them the power of choice to choose life or death, and blessing or cursing. (KJV-Deuteronomy 30:19) Counseling consists of three very important things: listening, repeating, and asking questioning. This doesn't mean you can't give advice it just means it's their choice to receive or reject your advice. Never make anyone feel guilty for rejecting your advice. That's his or her choice. When we take on the responsibility of making choices for others (children, Church members, wives, husbands etc.) we are taking on the burdens of living both their lives and ours.

This is not the will of God because if we try to take responsibility for others and make their choices it will eventually destroy both parties involved.

God gives us the answers in His word how to deal with all people that crosses our path in this life. For example He tells us how to train our children up in the way they should go and when they are old they want depart. He didn't say anything about living their life for them only to train them while they are children. Israel is a perfect example of a parent who tried to live his life through his children. He tried to hold on to both Joseph and Benjamin because of his love for his wife, Rachel. He never asked Benjamin, who was a grown man, did he want to go to Egypt. He just told his sons he wasn't sending him. Israel almost lost his blessing to feed his family because of the choice he had made for his son, Benjamin. Notice God never asked Israel about sending Joseph to Egypt because Joseph belonged to God, and He was the one who gave Israel his children.

We are just stewards over God's property. Israel finally had to surrender to God, and allow Benjamin to go with his brothers because he wasn't stronger than God or his plan that he had for his family. Remember we are bought with a price we are no longer our own. (KJV-I Corinthians 6:19,20) Counselors don't take it personally if someone rejects your advice or counseling, you did your part and that's all God requires of you. Did you know God gives a person the power of choice to choose Heaven or Hell, blessing or curses? (Deuteronomy 30:19) That is their "God given right" as a free mortal agent to choose to accept Jesus or reject Him.

The majority of people that comes to counselors just want someone to listen to them or lend them their ear. Counselors are supposed to be like a tape recorder that rewinds and repeats every word back to the person that he or she has said.

They asked the famous question "What do you want to do?" When this question is directed to the person it will give them back the power or control over their life. Adam blamed God for his disobedient, and Eve blamed the serpent.

The "Soul" is selfish, and it wants to be in control of the body, but doesn't want to take responsibility for its' actions. This is another reason why we must be careful in counseling people. First, most people want you to choose which direction they should take so they want have to be responsible if something goes wrong. Second, if something goes wrong they want to point the finger and blame you for their problems. I know what you are thinking suppose a person doesn't know what to do? Then you guide them in both the word of God and the law of the land. The key word is "Guide." The word "Guide" means you give them the information that they may not have to make a conscious decision, and then step back and allow them to choose.

We must remember that God is the one who know what's best for us. Even with that in mind He still gives us the power of choice. Deuteronomy 30:19-20 KJV "I call heaven and earth to record this day against you, that I have set before you, life and death, blessing and cursing: therefore choose life, that both thou and thy seed may live.

20 That thou mayest love the Lord thy God, and that thou mayest obey his voice, and that thou mayest cleave unto him: for he is thy life, and the length of thy days: that thou mayest dwell in the land which the Lord sware unto thy fathers, to Abraham, to Isaac, and to Jacob, to give them."

See the key word here is "Love." When we love God with all our heart, and with all our soul, and might we can choose life instead of death. (KJV-Deuteronomy 6:5) In this scripture the words "Heart, Soul, and Might" are involved. The word Heart is not used interchangeably with soul in this scripture as the writer sometimes uses it in scripture. The Heart here is the spirit of man and the Soul is what makes men self- conscious, and the word might means strength. So in this scripture it is saying something we have to do. We must put forth the effort to love God with our heart and command our soul to come in line with God's word. Then there is the word might that means strength and we are to use all the strength we have within us to love God.

David, the Prophet, put it this way in the Psalms: Bless the Lord, O my soul: and all that is within me, bless his holy name." (KJV-Psalms 103:1)

Chapter 9
Jesus, our Perfect Example

Jesus, our LORD, and Savior He is the perfect example for Christians who will walk in His footsteps. He yielded his "Will" totally to God. Jesus emptied Himself of his glory he had with the Father and took upon Himself the form of a servant. God, the Word, was God in the beginning, but he agreed to come to the Earth through a virgin and become a man made in the image of God. (John 1:1,2; Philippians 2:6-8; Galatians 4:4)
I Corinthians 15:45 KJV "And so it is written, The first man Adam was made a living soul; the last Adam was made a quickening spirit." I Corinthians 15:47 KJV "The first man is of the earth, earthy: the second man is the Lord from heaven." Notice the contrast between the two: The first Adam was made a living Soul and the last Adam, Jesus, was made a quickening spirit. Jesus is the one who quickens the spirits of men with His word. (John 5:21)
In spite of what people may believe, Jesus wasn't the second plan that God had He was the first. Revelation 13:8 KJV "And all that dwell upon the earth shall worship him, whose names are not written in the book of life of the Lamb slain from the foundation of the world." God, the Father, had already set his plan in motion to send Jesus to the earth to die for mankind from the foundation of the world. I like to put it this way; He came Himself through His Son, Jesus Christ.
II Corinthians 5:19 KJV says, "To wit, that God was in Christ, reconciling the world unto himself, not imputing their trespasses unto them; and hath committed unto us the word of reconciliation." Earlier in this book we talk about God establishing authority in the earth through obedience. We talked about two creatures: Lucifer, first ruler, of the Earth, and Adam, second ruler, of the Earth. They were an angelic creation of God and a Human being who was made in the image of God and after His likeness. Both were given a simple test, the test of obedience, and both failed.

Lucifer and the third part of the angels knew the choice that they were making was irreversible when they rebelled against God. God created angels individually and the choice they made was for eternity. There is no salvation for "Angels." If there was salvation for Lucifer and his fallen angels Christ would have had to die for every individual angel.

Praise God there is salvation for mankind. There were two representatives for the "Human Race", the first Adam and the Last Adam, Jesus Christ. The first Adam was the only man Elohim created. We come through blood ties, the reproduction of our parents. All die in Adam, and all those who accepts the last Adam, Jesus, as their Lord and Savior will live in Him. (Romans 5:12,15,17; I Corinthians 15:22,45)

Concerning Adam (man) God loved him, whom he had created in His own image, and after His likeness that he made a way of escape for us to be reconciled back to Him through His Son, Jesus. John 3:16 KJV "For God so loved the world, that he gave his only begotten Son, that whosoever believeth in him should not perish, but have everlasting life."

Adam, a spiritual being, had the power (ability) of God in him to pass his test and make the right choice, but instead he willingly chose to disobey God. When Adam made that choice he committed high treason. The word "Treason" means violation of allegiance toward one's country or sovereign, esp. the betrayal of one's own country by waging war against it or by consciously and purposely acting to aid its enemy.

I Timothy 2:13-14 KJV "For Adam was first formed, then Eve. 14 verse And Adam was not deceived, but the woman being deceived was in the transgression." Earlier in my book I said Adam wasn't omniscience. He didn't know about Satan, but God gave him all the information and power that he needed to pass his test. I have referred back to this statement many times in my book: God must establish His authority in the earth through obedience. A government can't operate properly where citizens disobey the laws of the land because it will create chaos in that country.

There was no man on the earth who could die for men because all men have sinned in Adam. (Romans 5:12) Ezekiel 22:30 KJV "And I sought for a man among them, that should make up the hedge, and stand in the gap before me for the land, that I should not destroy it: but I found none." I believe the Godhead bodily went into council and they came to an agreement that God, the Father, would send God, the Word, to the earth and he would be born through the Virgin, Mary, as God, the, Holy Ghost, overshadowed her womb. (KJV-Isaiah-7:14;Luke-1:30-35)

Hebrews-10:5-7-KJV "Wherefore when he cometh into the world, he saith, Sacrifice and offering thou wouldest not, but a body hast thou prepared me: 6 verse In burnt-offerings and sacrifices for sin thou hast had no pleasure. 7 "Then said I, Lo, I come (in the volume of the book it is written of me,) to do thy will, O God." When Adam disobeyed God his disobedience brought us into the bondage of sin.

We didn't have a choice in the matter as we didn't have a choice in being born; however we do have a choice through the last Adam, Jesus to be born-again.

Galatians 4:3-5 KJV says, "Even so we, when we were children, were in bondage under the elements of the world: 4 verse But when the fullness of the time was come, God sent forth his Son, made of a woman, made under the law, 5 verse To redeem them that were under the law, that we might receive the adoption of sons." In the meantime God in His love and Grace made "Covenants" with men until he could send Jesus through forty-two generations. (Matthew 1:17) God, the Creator, of Heaven and Earth made the "Edenic Covenant" with Adam. This was an agreement between "God" and "Adam." Adam broke the Covenant when he disobeyed God. We would call Adam today a "Traitor." He gave everything that God gave him over to Satan which is both God's archenemy and man. Satan, now is god of this world.

II Corinthians 4:4 KJV "In whom the god of this world hath blinded the minds of them which believe not, lest the light of the glorious gospel of Christ, who is image of God, should shine unto them."

When Adam disobeyed God it close the door in God's face in a manner of speaking. He was shut out of the Earth and Satan, who was an alien, in the Earth stole the dominion from Adam through deception. Satan was an alien because he wasn't a citizen of the Earth. To become a citizen of the Earth you have to be born here. Adam was the god of this world until he disobeyed and gave it over to Satan. When we disobeyed God we give our blessings over to Satan, and we lose ground with God.

Satan couldn't take anything away from Adam he had to deceive him in giving it up willingly. Christians, Satan can't take anything from us, but he can deceive us into giving the blessings of God away through our disobedience. You might ask the question; "Why didn't God take back the "Earth" from Satan?" It didn't belong to God because he gave Adam the dominion over the Earth. If God did that he would be a thief like Satan, but remember God is always in control. (John 10:10) Remember the title of the book "Yielding your will totally to God." The omniscience God already knew the choice both Lucifer and Adam would choose.

Even though God knew the condition of men's heart, and the chaos that sin would bring to his recreated Earth He wouldn't override Adam's "Will. If God did that he would become a dictator and man would be a robot, but he made him a free mortal agent.

God began to make "Covenants" with men to intervene back into the Earth so He could save mankind. John 3:16 is a verse in the Bible that most children can quote, but it is a powerful scripture. He loves us so much that he intervened in the Earth through Covenants with men until he could send His Son, Jesus through forty-two generations to redeem us back unto Himself. (KJV-Matthew 1:17;Galatians 3:13)

Satan couldn't shut God out of the Earth although he took over Adam's rule through deception. I believe God in His infinite wisdom gave Adam a lease over the Earth for only six thousand years. Didn't I tell you God is in control? Charles Capps, a great teacher, of the word of God said on one of his program that 120 times 50 Jubilee's equals 6000 years.

He quoted Genesis 6:3 KJV "And the Lord said, My spirit shall not always strive with man, for that he also is flesh: yet his days shall be an hundred and twenty years." I believe he said the count started during the year of Jubilee during the 50th year. Satan knows he has but a short time for his six thousand years is just about up. Revelation 12:12 KJV says, "Therefore rejoice, ye heavens, and ye that dwell in them. Woe to the inhabiters of the earth and of the sea! For the devil is come down unto you, having great wrath, because he knoweth that he hath but a short time."

I said early in the chapters that God accepted the blood of animals that men offered up as sacrifices. This was an act of their faith toward God to receive forgiveness for their sins. They also offer up sacrifices as Priests of their home until God established the Aaronic priesthood. Hebrews 10:10-13 KJV " By the which will we are sanctified through the offering of the body of Jesus Christ once for all. 11 verse And every priest standeth daily ministering and offering oftentimes the same sacrifices, which can never take away sins:
12 verse But this man, after he had offered one sacrifice for sins for ever, sat down on the right hand of God; 13 verse From henceforth expecting till his enemies be made his footstool."

Jesus was sent to the earth and given a body that he would become the ultimate sacrifice for mankind. He was the last Adam who came to gain back what the first Adam lost through disobedience. Romans 5:19 "For as by one man's disobedience many were made sinners, so by the obedience of one shall many be made righteous." Jesus must be tested also. Watchman nee said in his book, "Spiritual Authority": Jesus didn't bring obedience from heaven He learned it through the things He suffered.
Hebrews 5:8-10 KJV "Though he were a Son, yet learned he obedience by the things which he suffered; 9 verse And being made perfect, he became the author of eternal salvation unto all them that obey him; 10 verse Called of God an high priest after the order of Melchizedek."

51

Let's talk about "Jesus, our perfect example." Many people think because Jesus was the "Son of God" it wasn't a problem for Him to endure His hardships as a good solider. We must understand that though He was a Son, yet learned he obedience through the things He suffered. (Hebrews 5:8)

Philippians 2:5-8 "Let this mind be in you, which was also in Christ Jesus: 6 verse Who, being in the form of God, thought it not robbery to be equal with God: 7 verse But made himself of no reputation, and took upon him the form of a servant, and was made in the likeness of men: 8 verse And being found in fashion as a man, he humbled himself, and became obedient unto death, even the death of the cross."

We must get the full understanding concerning our Lord and Savior, Christ Jesus, He came as the Son of Man as Luke represented Him. The four Gospels represented the four sides of Jesus or it shows us the whole picture. Each Gospel represents Christ in His fullness. Ezekiel 1:10 KJV says, "As for the likeness of their faces, they four had the face of a man, and the face of a lion, on the right side: and they four had the face of an ox on the left side; they four also had the face of an eagle." I like to put it this way; Jesus was a hundred percent man and a hundred percent God. Jesus took on the form of a servant and humbled himself that he might die for mankind. He became obedient unto death even the death of the cross. (KJV-Philippians 2:5-8) Jesus was filled with the Spirit of God. (KJV-Luke 4:1)

He is the "Son of Man" who has a Spirit, Soul, and Body. (I Thessalonians 5:23) Paul, the Apostle, writes to the Galatians, "But when the fullness of time was come, God sent forth his Son, made of a woman, made under the law. 5verse To redeem them that were under the law, that we might receive the adoption of sons." (KJV-Galatians 4:4,5; Isaiah 7:14;Galatians 3:13)

I wanted to bring this to your attention because we must see Jesus, as the "Son of Man." Everything Jesus, received from God while He, was on the earth to live a victorious life He has given it to us in Christ. "These things I have spoken unto you, that in me ye might have peace.

In the world ye shall have tribulation: but be of good cheer; I have overcome the world." (KJV-St. John 16:33)

Now that that has been established let's go on to know the Lord. The twenty-six chapter of Matthew shows us Jesus in His weakest and most crucial stage of His life as the "Son of Man" when He was in the "Garden of Gethsemane." This is where he gained the victory through prayer that gave him the strength to endure the cross.

Matthew 26:39 KJV "And he went a little further, and fell on his face, and prayed, saying, O my Father, if it be possible, let this cup pass from me: nevertheless not as I will, but as thou wilt." Jesus, the Son of Man's, flesh was warring against the spirit and he began to pray to the Father; if it be possible, let this cup pass from me: nevertheless not as I will, but as thou wilt."

Jesus, came to the Earth to be the sacrificial lamb, who would John seeth Jesus coming unto him, and saith, Behold the Lamb of God, which taketh away the sin of the world." I believe when Jesus, our Savior, was on the mount of Transfiguration Elisha and Moses told him he would die for the sins of the world. (KJV-Matthew 17:1-3`)

This is not scripture, but this is my theory. I don't believe God would have revealed this to Jesus when he was growing up as a young man. God reveals and prepares us for ministry and gives us the grace we need to fulfill our destiny one step at a time. We know it is revealed to Jesus that he has to die for mankind whenever or however God revealed it to Him. He prays and asked His father to take this cup from Him. Jesus, as the Son of Man, had the choice to die for mankind or he could have chosen not too. This is scary when we think about it, but thank God, Jesus loved us so much that He endured the cross. (Hebrews 12:2) He won the victory over the flesh in the "Garden of Gethsemane." (Matthew 26:36). John10:17,18 KJV "Therefore doth my father love me, because I lay down my life, that I might take it again. 18verse No man taketh it from me, but I lay it down, and I have power to take it again." This commandment have I received of my father." We must understand that Jesus, was God, the Word, who created everything in the Heavens and in the Earth.

Colossians 1:15 KJV says, " Who is the image of the invisible God, the firstborn of every creature: 16 verse For by him were all things created, that are in heaven, and that are in earth, visible and invisible, whether they be thrones, or dominions, or principalities, or powers: all things were created by him, and for him." Imagine just for a moment that you are God and you created all things and were born into the earth to redeem your creation and they crucified you. They marred Jesus until he didn't even look like a human being.

Isaiah 52:14 KJV says, "As many were astonished at thee, his visage was so marred more than any man, and his form more than the sons of men." Jesus yielded his will totally to God's will and gave his life a ransom for the sin of the world. (Mark 10:45) Watchmen Nee in his book "Spiritual Authority" said there was two ways for Jesus to return to heaven: one way was to obey absolutely and unreservedly as man, establishing the authority of God in all things on all occasions without the slightest hint of rebellion; thus step by step through obedience to God, He would be Lord over all.

The other way would be to force his way back by reclaiming and using the authority and power and glory of His deity because of having found obedience impossible through the weakness and limitation of human flesh. Thank God He discarded this second path and walked humbly in the way of obedience- even unto death.

Sources

Nee Watchmen.   Spiritual Authority.   Copyright ©
1972 by Christian Fellowship Publishes, INC.

New Scofield Study System.   Editor C.I. Scofield,D.D.
New York: Copyright© 1967, 1978 by Oxford
University Press, INC.

www.ingramcontent.com/pod-product-compliance
Lightning Source LLC
Chambersburg PA
CBHW051711090426
42736CB00013B/2653